Get Noticed!

Resume & Career advice to make you stand out!

by James Grimm

Contact James at hro.jim@gmail.com

Follow Jame's blog: http://jegrimm.wordpress.com

Facebook Resume page:
http://www.facebook.com/resumencareerbyjim

Amazon Author Page: http://amazon.com/author/book4jim

Copyright © 2019 James Grimm

All Rights Reserved

Keywords: (Resume/ Career)

This book is made possible with the assistance of the following people. Thank you very much for your input, story, and responses!

Reiko Motobu, Emily Burns, Akiko Kuroki, Helen Zhou, Ellen Grace Olleres, SeungHyun Kim, Lisa Arai, and Richard Grimm

Table of Contents

INTRODUCTION 7

The Achievement 8
Example of an Achievement 8
What makes up an Achievement 10
How to write an Achievement 13
Other considerations 18
Validating your Achievements 20
What if I do not believe I have any Achievements? 26
Should I stop at three Achievements per position? 28

The Resume 30
Resume template & style 30

Job Search Tips 40
Cover Letters 40
What about significant time gaps between jobs 42
A lot of jobs with little time at each one 43
Interview hints 45
When should I tell my boss when I quit? 47
Do I need to draft a resignation letter? 48
What if they give me a counter-offer? 49

Career Tips 51

Email address 51
  LinkedIn..52
  Social Network Sites (SNS)..53
  Networking 53
  Burning bridges..53
  Hiring pay 54
  Pay raises once hired..55
  Toot your own horn 56
  Innovation 57
  Going forward 58
  When is it time to move on? 60
  Trying a new job field 62
  What if a job does not end well.....................................63

Conclusion 66

Appendix A..67
  Resume from 1998..67
  Resume from 2004..70
  Resume from 2010..74
  Resume from 2019..79

INTRODUCTION

Why write this book? My answer is to help you learn how to write a resume that interests your readers. Also, to provide career advice that will help you fill that resume with hard-hitting achievements.

Over the last few years, I have seen a large number of resumes and the majority of them were very disappointing. These resumes rarely gave the reader a good indication of the person's skill set. When a reader has many candidates, with none standing out, it is pretty much a guessing game.

With over two decades of IT experience in eight different companies, I have seen many different ways people want to see a resume. My first resumes listed software tools or equipment I had used. The listing of skills was the primary way to do things in the early "scan the resume into a database" days. Today that does not seem to be as prevalent. Some recruiters and companies still prefer that, but the scanning software and database searching tools have gotten better.

You see, the majority of resumes I have seen are still showing tasks, software tools, or equipment but not scope. How do I know if the candidate can handle the complexity of what I need doing? How do I know whether they can barely do the job or are a superstar?

With vague, generic statements, I might as well put all those resumes in a box and pick one. It almost comes down to, "... you've got to ask yourself one question: "Do I feel lucky?" Well, do ya, punk? " - Dirty Harry.

This book discusses how to present your skills in a way that gives the reader a good measure of what you are capable of handling. Hopefully, get you an interview before they have to pick resumes randomly. This book also offers general career advice and explanations of how the hiring process works from my observations.

The Achievement

Chapter One

The first thing I suggest is to have a current resume. Pretty standard advice, and it makes sense. You never know when you will find yourself looking for another job. Additionally, it doesn't hurt to occasionally test the waters of the job market to see if you can improve your situation or, if nothing else, to find your value in the job market.

To do this, you need to figure out what skills you can offer a potential employer. In my opinion, this is best done by showing your achievements. What is an achievement? Is it a listing of what tasks you work on and job skills? No. An achievement is a summary of something significant you have done during your employment in that position.

Think of these achievements as something you would brag to peers or friends about how you do your job. When you are bragging, you do not talk about your daily work unless that is incredibly interesting. No, you talk about things that go above and beyond or how you do more than everyone else in the same job. An achievement, like bragging, typically would not list all the actions of your position but would highlight something you did that you think others have not done.

Example of an Achievement

So let's start by showing an example of what I am suggesting. Below you will see a pattern similar to many resumes I have seen. While I am an IT guy by trade, what I am suggesting works for any field. Throughout this book, I will overwhelmingly use IT examples. I will try to add others to give our non-IT readers a chance to visualize achievements. Not as many as I would like, but I will try.

Not an achievement bullet - *Bartender, makes drinks, and works the cash register.*

What does this tell you about the person? That they worked at a bar, but what else? What was the size of the bar? Maybe it is a popular restaurant or bar chain, you would have a good idea of the scale. Perhaps not. It could be a tiny bar that has a few seats or a large establishment that the bartender is always making drinks. We don't know from this statement. Can they handle making specialty cocktails or making hundreds of drinks a shift? Again we can not tell. They can take in money but do they close the books at the end of the night? Make supply orders? How about how well they do the job? Nothing else sticks out with this statement.

Achievement bullet - *Senior bartender serving an average of 400 drinks, bringing in over 2000 dollars a night. Closing manager four nights a week. Awarded employee of the month four times in 19 months.*

How does this differ from the previous example? It provides scope by quantifying the amount of work done. With 400 drinks a night, we know how busy the bar is. Depending on the bar, this might show the candidate can work well under pressure. The candidate has also been recognized by their company for performance and is trusted enough to close the facility.

Which candidate would you want to call first?

> **TIP: Hiring managers usually are time-constrained in going through large numbers of resumes. The goal is to make it easier for the hiring manager to have a positive impression by providing enough information in your resume that differentiates you from the pack.**

Why is it essential to write a bullet this way? With the first example, the hiring manager would not know which candidates have experience working in an environment similar to the one they have. If you received fifty resumes looking like this, the hiring company would have to call many candidates and try to figure out what amount of work the candidate did. There is a good chance they will become fatigued with the process and might choose someone that 'might' meet the job description. If they saw a resume like the second example, they would probably call that candidate before calling any of those that looked like the first example. The goal is to be the person that writes like the second example.

> **TIP: The hiring process is an additional duty that the hiring manager has to do, and not always one they consider fun. There is the added stress of hiring someone wrong for the job. An open position also means that others in the team have to do additional work. Your goal is to make it easy for them to feel you are the right candidate.**

What makes up an Achievement

The first thing to do is to create a list of achievements. Don't worry about grammar or length at this point. It's a draft. Do this for each job you have held. Try to have at least three or four items per post but do as many as you can. Later you can select which are best to represent you.

When writing an achievement, think about what you did for this accomplishment. An achievement's summary should describe your role, what you did, the complexity, and the value of the work. Also, you can mention if you received any awards or positive feedback for your contribution.

Consider writing the achievement similar to what you would say when bragging to a group of your peers. Write it as if you are talking to people that do the same type of work. If you told your peers, "Ya, I'm a Data Center manager." Maybe some thoughtful responses, but if you said, "Ya, I'm a Data Center manager at <Company name>'s cloud service data center." Alternatively, something like, "I manage a 1000 rack Data Center for <Company name>." These statements further clarify and give the listener more to work with to understand the size and complexity of what you do.

Moreover, like with bragging, the key is to be the last one to "one-up" the others. In the resume world, this means that your resume provides the best information, and it is the type of information the reader is looking to find. If everyone can say they are a Data Center (DC) manager, then it provides no value when considering how to make you stand out. Adding that you managed a 1000 rack DC would then beat out anyone that led a smaller DC or didn't quantify their position. So right away, you have raised the bar and positioned yourself above those mentioning smaller data centers or not quantifying or qualifying at all. If you keep doing things like that with your achievements, then you should get the call, and the others might only if you fail to impress on the call.

> **TIP: It would be much easier if you get in the habit of always doing this. If you worked on a project, summarize your contribution and the scope right after you completed it. Much easier to remember what you have done right afterward, than a year or two later.**
>
> **TIP: This can also contribute to your evaluations at your company. Writing this up can help you write your promotion document or give you speaking points to use during discussions with your manager.**

Another example. I helped a friend with her resume, who reworked her company's mobile phone contracts. The result was a significant saving in the contract. In her original resume, she just listed that she provided savings by renegotiating the mobile phone contract. I did not know the significance of it until I asked her to explain it. After learning about the number of phones involved and the savings she was able to negotiate, we rewrote the bullet.

The way it was initially written would show no difference with someone that took care of a much smaller number of phones and saved a lesser amount of money. She was managing around one thousand phones and saved nearly one hundred thousand dollars over the contract.

Quantify or qualify your achievements as much as possible. It gives the reader a chance to rank you against your peers. Going forward, I will refer to quantify or qualify as 2Qs. Corny, but hopefully, it sticks in your mind and becomes something you always look to do when creating achievements.

The more questions you can answer about your skills and accomplishments in the resume, the more likely an interview. Remember what I said earlier about bragging. Once you use 2Qs in the achievement, you are throwing down the gauntlet and challenging others to show they are better. Vague statements listing your skills or tasks you perform do not provide the same challenge.

Many people can say they serve drinks, make sales, fix PCs, manage people, etc. The thing that can set you apart before the interview is by showing numbers or explaining the task or accomplishment's importance. Sounding repetitive, don't I? Sorry but this is the key to what I am saying. 2Qs your achievements and things start to fall into place.

Another friend asked me to help him write his resume. He was a car salesperson and wanted to try something different. He had a lot of material to work with but was not using 2Qs to bring out the significance of the statements.

After a few beers and many probing questions, we found out his team increased their sales volume and revenue generated. He did not mention it in his resume. They are now. He also was making a lot of sales himself. Again something he did not list in his resume. Something a potential hiring manager would love to know about the person they are considering to hire, especially if they are in a sales team.

See folks, 2Qs is the act of further explaining why you thought something was important enough to put down on your resume. Why does it matter? Without using 2Qs, so what? Okay, the broken record will kinda, sorta stop now.

One last note. Throughout this book, I will mention "the reader." When I say this, I mean the potential hiring manager and others in the company that is involved in the hiring process. This includes someone in Human Resources (HR), the hiring manager, and a few of your future peers or others in the process. I have seen many different hiring processes in my previous companies.

How to write an Achievement

Let's break this down.

Role + What you did + Environment + Value to the company = Achievement

One thing to note. Achievements need to show complexity and value to the company. If you can not express both of those points, you don't have the strongest of accomplishments to discuss. Probably need to go back and think about it some more to find the missing components.

What was your role?

When we say your role, we are discussing your role in the achievement. For example, you could be a desktop technician and take on the project coordinator role for this achievement. Not all companies use dedicated project managers; thus, this might be what you took on for this particular project.

If it is different than your typical job's role, it would be a benefit to mention. It shows you have experience in this type of work. Additionally, it shows you are flexible and able to work beyond your standard job description. If your role for this achievement was in line with your job at the company, you could skip mentioning this part.

What did you do?

When you explain what you did, use action verbs as much as possible. It is best if you were the one that led the project, developed the solution, submitted the proposal, or identified the problem. Not just for resume writing, but do these in your career!

Looking at a resume and seeing an achievement that explains the complexity but doesn't identify what role you played is a red flag. If you were on a team that built something noteworthy, that is great. However, what was your efforts towards that project? That is what the reader would like to know. Remember, they are considering to hire you and not your whole project team.

The key is to make it short. No long explanations are necessary. If it takes more than a sentence to explain, it probably is too long unless it is a phenomenal accomplishment.

What was the complexity of the Achievement?

With this component, you need to show why this matters. The goal is to show the reader your experience operating in complex or challenging environments or situations. This is where the need to use 2Qs comes into play.

This component is not to be confused with the last element of the achievement. This part sets the stage for how cool the discussed item's environment was during the period. In other words, the bragging rights part of the equation.

This item is not the value of sales that you achieved, nor the revenue the company generated from what you helped create. What this element is, is to qualify (Enterprise, Government, new customer) or quantify (number of customers, percent of sales goal) how these sales count.

Another way to show the complexity is by listing the financial value of the tools or the environment. If the achievement describes the company spending 1,000 dollars to put in something, the expertise required will be one level. If the value is ten million dollars, then the complexity is much higher. People in the industry know the tasks necessary for industry-standard items.

Remember, even if the "wow" value is not that great, it might be more significant than the experience of your competition. So don't get depressed if you feel your achievements are not overwhelming.

Here are some examples of value to give you an idea;

When building, the size of what you made.	When moving, the weight and value of the items moved.	The value of the reviewed material and length of time to study.
When managing; the number of people and size of the area of responsibility.	When repairing systems, the size, value, complexity, importance to the company.	When programming, the # of lines of code, transactions, connections, complexity, the value of transactions.
For customer support, the number of calls compared against your peers, satisfaction rating.	For retail sales, the number of customers helped or the value of the products sold and feedback.	For facilities, the value of the property or inventory you manage.

If you wish, you could also list the skills you used in this accomplishment. I would not get carried away by mentioning every type of skill or tool used. Nor would I list company-specific tools since others might not know what they are. We will discuss this below.

What is the value of this to your company?

This is where you bring it all together. The "money shot" if you will. This element is how you show the reader how your actions brought value to the company. Think about it. What the reader really wants to know is how you might bring value to their company. It could be as simple as "are you a good fit" for the team to something more like, if your listed achievements show you are an innovator, "Can she invent for my company too?"

Put a value on your work. Some questions to ask about your achievements:

- If you sell things, this is where you would mention the value of the sold product or services.

- If you implemented a new service, this is where you would mention the benefits of that service.

- If you proposed a new solution, this is where you mention the benefit or cost savings of that solution.

Any positive recognition or awards for this Achievement?

While this is rare, at least with me, I have also quoted positive correspondence or mentioned awards. If you do list written praise, please include the title of the person in the bullet. I would not add this component unless it is a senior member of management endorsing your efforts. For awards, again, it is up to you. One Tech of the Quarter in a job you held for four years is probably not something you want to mention. Think about it, rare recognition, while helpful, does not show your previous companies recognize you unless it occurs often enough to show consistent above-average performance. If you are receiving this once or twice a year, every year you are there, that is significant.

If the award is for your efforts in the accomplishment, then add it.

If the award is to the team without specifically mentioning your contributions, I would probably not use it. Additionally, if it lists out all members without their contributions, it is not an award for your efforts.

Listing an award is more window dressing on the achievement, so do not spend a lot of page space explaining it. There are exceptions. Use your judgment when you should devote more space to describing the award.

Other considerations

Now you know the generalities of creating accomplishments, here are a few notes to remember.

It is a good idea to make sure you know if the name of the tools you use are industry standards or unique to the company. Sometimes the name used by your company (or military) might be different than what is elsewhere. In these cases, it might be best to provide a generic name for the type of tool, like "inventory tool."

Along with industry-standard naming conventions, think about other 'jargon' used at your location that might not be the same elsewhere. When I was in the Navy, we used "watch section" to mean "shift." Many large companies or government jobs have a whole list of terms they use that another organization would not understand. Research on the web to find the standard industry terms used.

> **TIP: Do not overly concern yourself with getting the exact name or function of all of the tools you worked with (nomenclatures or sub-parts). The reader is more concerned with your usage of the tools and not the exact name. If you do find a job description that lists specific tools in exacting detail, then yes, it would be something to consider. Most people will ask more at the interview and would like to know if you have an understanding of how a type of tool works.**

Please do not write down items that are confidential or propriety to that company. You can refer to things, but make sure you follow the agreement you signed with that company. There is usually a way to write and not to give away any secrets.

Here are some examples:

> *Developed a concept to create a secure means to handle and track used storage media within data centers. Currently, in the prototyping stage. The idea received a regional Kaizen award.*

> *Submitted an idea about drone usage in warehouses. It was selected for further development as a finalist idea in the annual company-wide innovation competition for 2018. One of 289 ideas from nearly 3000 that was judged and chosen by the senior leadership team. Additionally, submitted nine other ideas and ranked 22 of 578 volunteer judges for the competition's initial judging phase.*

> *Submitted an invention for a cable solution that uses photon emissions to detect cable damage.*

It should go without saying, but please be honest with the numbers and your contributions. You will most likely discuss these during interviews. So make sure you can talk confidently about what you claim.

Another good source of bullets to add is received awards. The award as the achievement, not a component of one. If you received 'salesperson of the month' or year, these would be outstanding bullets but consider the period these covered. As mentioned above, a Salesperson of the Month for one month out of many years is probably not the best example. Being the Salesperson of the Month ten times in four years and maybe of the year once, would be an outstanding achievement. Remember to treat this as an achievement, as we discuss above. You need to show how this shows value to the company and use 2Qs. Try to include costs or numbers, like the number of your peers, the number of transactions you handled, or the percentage of your goal achieved. If you are part of a twenty-person sales force or a 100 person call center, these can give the reader an idea of how difficult it is to be recognized.

Something like:

> *Awarded Salesperson of the Month ten times and Salesperson of the Year once in four years, bringing in over one million dollars in revenue. Included in the top five of a twenty-person sales force for the entire period.*

You can shorten the text more when it is in the context of your resume, but I lengthened it to make it understandable as a stand-alone item.

Validating your Achievements

So you have created your list of accomplishments. Now what? I would put the document away for a few days. Preferably a week or two. The idea is to get some distance from your writing of these bullets. When you look at them again, you want to have an objective view of them. Over the period you have been away from this list, you will have forgotten some of the subconscious explanations you have used to tell yourself the achievement is solid. Remember, most folks tend to think things about the complete thought and miss a few things when writing it down. Your mind literally fills in the gaps because it knows what you wanted to say. Thus giving yourself some time away from the writing is good and will help you find the glaring holes you most likely have in some, if not all, of the bullets.

An excellent way to see if there is value in the achievement is to ask yourself these questions:

1. What did I do?
2. Why does that matter?
3. How complicated was the task?
4. What value did it provide my company?
5. BONUS: Did my company recognize my contribution?

Let's look at the bartender example again:

Senior bartender serving an average of 400 drinks bringing in over 2000 dollars a night. Awarded employee of the month four times in 19 months. Acts as closing manager four nights a week.

1) **What did I do?**

Answer: I was a bartender.

2) **Why does that matter?**

Answer: I was a senior bartender working at a busy bar.

3) **How complicated was the task?**

Answer: I made over 400 drinks a night, closed the bar, ordered supplies, and handled money.

4) **What value did this provide the company?**

Answer: I made over 2000 dollars a night for the company.

5) **Did my company recognize my contribution?**

Answer: I was awarded employee of the month four times in 19 months.

You should be able to answer most of these questions with solid answers that can impress someone in the industry. If you can not, then maybe you need to develop this bullet further, or this is not a strong bullet to include in your resume. This is one of the reasons to create more achievement bullets than you plan on putting on your resume. Some might not work when you come back to review them, or some are better in different situations.

Here are some other examples of achievement bullets:

Example One:

Led the migration project for upgrading the BlueCoat proxy systems in Tokyo. Developed the migration plan for 120+ applications for a 700+ user base. Migration was successfully implemented without significant issues.

Questions:

1) What did I do?

Answer: Lead engineer that developed the migration plan for the BlueCoat systems.

2) Why does that matter?

Answer: It was a very involved process that was completed successfully without issue.

3) How complicated was the task?

Answer: The number of applications and users made this a significant project. Any application that failed would not be accessible to the users.

4) What value did this provide the company?

Answer: New functionality on newer systems with no significant issues to users.

5) Did my company recognize my contribution?

Answer: Nothing of significance.

Example Two:

Lead network engineer on the consolidation of offices in Seoul, Beijing, Chengdu, and Tokyo. Designed and installed the networks, utilizing Cisco Catalyst 6500 switches, c3845 ISR routers for MPLS WAN connectivity with DMVPN encryption tunnels. Seoul was noted as "This is the smoothest move in a long time," Senior Manager, Global Infrastructure Services.

Questions:

1) What did I do?

Answer: I was the lead engineer on some office build-outs.

2) Why does that matter?

Answer: Shows my skills in network design and planning plus experience with certain types of network equipment.

3) How complicated was the task?

Answer: It required me to design the network and install/configure the systems.

4) What value did this provide the company?

Answer: It helped the company get these sites online, allowing the users to work with the rest of the company.

5) Did my company recognize my contribution?

Answer: I included a positive quote that my management gave me at that time.

Example Three:

Through data analysis of mail usage records, discovered and proposed cost savings up to 40 million JPY per year.

Questions:

1) What did I do?

Answer: Analyzed mail records.

2) Why does that matter?

Answer: This was a saving that was not identified by others. We were migrating from on-site Microsoft Exchange to Office365 mail. I was going through the records to determine the order of migration by site and noticed old records that we didn't need to migrate.

3) How complicated was the task?

Answer: This was a migration for over 11,000 mailboxes with about 1,000 old user mailboxes. So I was going through the data to determine what was there, then calculated the cost in migration efforts and record storage. In other words, a lot of counting. I also had to draft up the proposal justifying what I was suggesting.

TIP: I was a technical project manager during this achievement. It was not my responsibility to go beyond the site migration order. I took the initiative to delve further and come up with the idea that we could save migration time and costs if we did not migrate the old mailboxes. This is the kind of 'above and beyond' actions that would get you recognized.

4) What value did this provide the company?

Answer: 40 million yen savings (approximately 400,000 USD).

5) Did my company recognize my contribution?

Answer: Nothing of significance.

TIP: Writing out the answers to these questions could give you good talking points when it comes time to discuss these in an interview. All this information does not need to be in the bullet, but if they ask you to explain the bullet, it will help you tell the story.

Once you have completed vetting your list of achievements, it is time to edit them to clean them up. Remember, the goal is to have an easy to read resume that shows what value you can bring to a potential employer. To do this, you need to clean up the achievements to use as few words as possible.

When writing bullets, complete sentences, or in-depth explanations are not necessary. Short, concise statements are best. If you notice in many of the examples, I try to remove the personal references because this should all be about you. This is not the way to write a report or cover letter, but for resumes, I have not had anyone complain to me. One to three sentences is acceptable, with one being optimal.

Take our bartender example:

Senior bartender serving an average of 400 drinks bringing in over 2000 dollars a night. Awarded employee of the month four times in 19 months. Acts as closing manager four nights a week.

Shorten to:

Senior bartender and closing manager serves an average of 400 drinks worth 2000 dollars a night. Employee of month four times.

This still tells the same information but with fewer words. The time is implicit in the start/stop dates of the Work Experience entry for this job. Alternatively, you could create a separate bullet for the Employee of the Month information if you had the number of employees and any specifics related to why you earned that award.

Something like:

Senior bartender and closing manager serves an average of 400 drinks worth 2000 dollars a night.

Earned Employee of the Month four times in 19 month period from an employee base of 60 employees.

What does this do? It separates this into two bullets. Conceivably, this could be all you had in this job. Now, instead of one bullet for the job, you have two bullets. Saying the same thing with the addition of a little more information also makes it sound a lot more impressive. Winning the award more than 20% of the time against 59 other employees speaks volumes of your efforts and how the company felt about you. You are spelling things out that some busy hiring managers might miss. This is good since you are guiding the conversation.

On the other hand, if you can not shrink the bullet without compromising what you are trying to say, then stick with the longer one.

What if I do not believe I have any Achievements?

What if you do not have any achievements that you think has value? Not the best, but fear not. Think about your responsibilities. This is what many will need to consider until you get in the habit of working towards making achievements.

What was the scope of your work? If you are a person that does not think they have any unique accomplishments, consider the total of what you do. How many customers do you serve? How many tickets do you close? Most companies have a list of metrics they use to determine who is doing what. These metrics can be used to help show the potential employers what you are capable of doing.

There is an excellent chance that the metrics your company uses are the same ones other companies with similar jobs use. So mentioning these metrics could be a positive thing. The hiring manager might be able to compare you to their current workers and get a feel for where you would fit in.

Things like:

- The number of servers you maintain.
- The number of customers you manage.
- The number of customers that come to your shop.
- Type of reports you create.
- Type of client you support.
- Value of property you manage.
- The number of transactions your software handles per day/second/hour.
- Type and number of equipment you manage.
- Size of territory you cover.
- The number of records you maintain.
- Value of your sales.
- Meeting group or individual goals.
- People you train or manage.
- Doing things on time or under budget.
- The number of positions you can handle.

Hopefully, you get the point. These can all be acceptable bullets. The idea is to show the amount of work you do. Look at item one, how many servers you maintain. If you manage 100 servers, that is different than if you manage 1000 servers.

A bullet for this could be:

Manage and repair 1000 servers across two data centers in support of the company's e-commerce site. Maintain a 100TB backup solution and monitoring for these systems.

The second sentence could even be a separate bullet if there is a lot of complexity involved. Notice how I mentioned the size of the backup solution. Adding numbers to the things you do will show your proficiency and workload. The goal would be to show how much you can handle.

> **TIP: Not all positions are looking for the person that has done the most of that type of job. An example, a manager looking for a technician to handle their 100 server data center might not prefer someone that works with thousands of servers. They might think that person will quickly get bored.**

Should I stop at three Achievements per position?

No, write as many achievements as you can. Put them all through the five-question criteria to weed out weak ones. These achievements might not make the current resume cut but might be more valuable if you try to change the job-type you are trying to get.

In my career, I have worked as a network engineer, technical support engineer, network monitoring administrator, project manager, IT architect, desktop team manager, and cloud data center manager. Depending on the job I am applying for, I sometimes modify the achievements.

For a project manager role, I emphasize the projects that I coordinated. For a manager position, the teams I managed, and proposals submitted that cut costs or improved efficiency.

To summarize, writing achievements using 2Qs will give readers a sense of how you can contribute to their company. Most people now and probably for the foreseeable future, will list tasks for most of their resume. By writing achievements using 2Qs, your resume will stand out over the competition by quantifying and qualifying what you are capable of accomplishing.

The Resume

Chapter Two

Now that we have the achievements organized, time to work on the resume. The first thing to remember is that most readers spend a short amount of time on your resume before they make an initial impression. A good rule of thumb is that the first half page of your resume should get them excited. If they do not get excited by then, they probably won't give the rest of your resume their full attention if they even read it.

Tons of books, blogs, and resume writing gurus suggest different ways to build your resume. No matter which style you like, they all should work towards this one goal, a resume's job is to get you an interview. What I discuss in this book is the one that I have used and have seen the most.

Is it better than other types? Not sure, but it works for me and the folks I have helped.

Resume template & style

I am not one for creative resumes since they are typically not computer search-friendly. They look cool with sidebars and other 'interesting' formatting schemes, but sometimes these creative templates make it more challenging to read. The goal is to pique the interest of the reader, to get an interview, not frustrate the reader. I imagine some creative jobs would appreciate a fancy resume, but most probably not.

I would also suggest a reverse chronological resume (last job first). Functional resumes are generally seen as trying to hide something. They might be suitable for someone that has been out of the workforce for a long break (like parents coming back after raising children) but are best not used by most job seekers. This book will talk exclusively about reverse chronological resumes.

The main thing to remember is to make your resume easy on the eyes. This means include a lot of white space. I have not even looked at resumes that look like a book's page (a page with very little white space). It is just hard on the eyes, and if you have been looking at a lot of resumes or are busy, it is a groan generating type of resume.

How long should it be? I don't think it matters if you have a lot of useful information. Making it readable (lots of white space) and having impacting achievements will be what people want. No one wants to read a few pages listing task after task without anything discussing how well the candidate can do these tasks. So shorter is better, especially if you have few achievements to consider.

The one rule I use is to have full pages. If you end up with less than a half-page of data, then find ways to shorten summaries or reduce some white space to remove that partial page or add more to make it over a half-page. I would suggest shortening since adding fluff is not in your best interest.

Another good rule of thumb is not to include achievements for jobs that do not pertain to your desired job-type. If you think it might add value, then okay, but do not spend too much time on those jobs. Additionally, if you have a long history of work, for us older folks, maybe include only one achievement or just a statement of the type of work done in those earlier positions.

What is an example of something outside of the field? I have written a fictional book and added that as a job that I did during a break between jobs. That has been a great ice breaker. So explaining a unique or exciting position that does not pertain to the one you are trying to get can be beneficial.

Contact Information

First is the contact information. There are many different thoughts on how to do this. At least have your name and contact method. I also put in an address and Email address, but it is not required. I do know that I and many others look at the name and address to try and visualize who you are. So too much information can distract the reader or give them an initial impression. Sad but true.

Summary of Skills

Next, I like to add a SUMMARY OF SKILLS. Going back to the idea that you have the first half-page to impress them, a SUMMARY OF SKILLS can get them excited and want to read more. This summary should be four to ten short bullets. Go through your achievements and pick the best. Shorten them to one line, if possible, and put here. Make sure what you put here is also mentioned elsewhere in your resume. You say here but explain in other parts of the resume.

This is also a great place to list certifications that are eye-catchers in your industry. Not every certification but top ones or ones that are needed to get the job you want. Listing languages is also beneficial if that matters to your industry. If you include languages and have a certification for that, then include or list native. If you only speak one language, do not include it.

It is best to try and include 2Qs in these statements, but not if you have to write a lengthy comment. As with so many rules, there are exceptions to this, as well. If you think it will add to the excitement, then a little longer will not hurt. Just try not to do for each bullet. Remember, it should be expanded upon in the Work Experience area.

Here are some samples of summaries I have used on my resumes.

- *WAN and LAN architect/engineer experienced in trading floor build-outs, global MPLS WANs, High-Frequency Trading networks, compute farm networks, virtual desktop initiatives, data center moves, and office build-outs.*

- *Managed an international IT operations team, cloud data center teams, and naval special intelligence communications shifts.*
- *Managed cloud service data centers with up to one thousand racks and up to 24,000 physical servers.*
- *Over 25 years of IT and communications experience in management, IT architect, data center management, network security officer, network and system administration to technical support.*
- *Designed and managed the fault and capacity management system for an S&P 500 corporation.*
- *Experienced at analyzing and correlating data, with a knack for discovering inefficiencies that can save money.*
- *Cisco Certified Network Administrator, ID: CSCOxxxxxx - June 2003.*
- *VMware Technical Sales Professional 5 – October 2013.*
- *Almost 14 years of U.S. Naval service with a TOP SECRET/Special Background clearance.*
- *Wrote and published a fictional book.*
- *Experienced in BlueCoat Proxy Systems; NetScout RMON probes; Cisco Catalyst switches, routers, PIX, ASA and Call Manager applications; Juniper WXC/Peribit WAN Optimization devices and SRX firewalls; Aruba Wireless controllers; MPLS/BGP/DMVPN/EIGRP; System Administration: Windows server 2003 and 2008, Redhat Linux, Solaris, HPUX, VMware and Citrix XenDesktop. Others: ITIL v2 & v3 and TQL*

Work Experience

After SUMMARY OF SKILLS, list your WORK EXPERIENCE. This is where you record each job with the current or last position first. Include company name/location, time frame employed, the title of your post, a short description of the job, and then the achievements. Some resumes have jobs where they do not list the company. I would highly recommend not following this practice because it could give the wrong impression. People do make assumptions about the level of work by the name of the company too. If you do not name the company but have some impressive achievements, it calls into question the legitimacy of the accomplishments.

Make sure your title is the official title of your position. You can find out from your human resources department if it was not on your initial contract. This is important because if a company checks your work history and your title is different, it can cause problems for your employment. I had seen someone that stated they were a network engineer when their official title was network administrator. The hiring company thought that meant a junior position that did less complex work than an engineer. The person almost lost the job because they were accused of providing false information. Best not to put yourself in that spot.

For your time employed, list month and year. That should suffice for most, if not all, companies. What I suggest should look like this:

<Company Name> March 2008 – April 2010

Network Engineer, Global Financial Services

Tokyo, Japan

Assigned to the <Customer Name> account for network implementations, primarily in Tokyo and Seoul. Responsible for design and implementation of router and switch expansions, blade chassis, and third party network (TPNC) implementations. Perform as 3rd line support for Tokyo NOC.

If you have multiple positions in a company with different achievements, create a group heading with the company name and total years in the company. Then drop down to each title with their achievements and time worked there. You should provide a separate job description per title.

Something like this:

<Company Name>: March 1998 – February 2008

(2006 – Feb08) Network Engineer, Global Infrastructure Service

Tokyo, Japan

Network engineer that managed the company's growing Asian-Pacific network infrastructure.

(2000 – 2006) Network Engineer, Global Infrastructure Service

Heathrow, Florida

Network engineer that managed the corporate network infrastructure, primarily, in the United States. As a network engineer, maintained router and switch configurations, provided network architecture and installation services, and troubleshot LAN/WAN problems.

(1998 – 2000) NerveCenter Senior Support Specialist, Technical Support

Heathrow, Florida

Provided configuration and customization support to customers of the NerveCenter product line.

The job description should be one or two sentences. Make it general statements that describe the scope of the job. It is up to you if you wish to quantify or qualify the scope here or create a bullet under this title. If you have plenty of achievements under this position, you can add the scope to the description.

If you have worked a period of only consulting, contract, or part-time work with many clients, I would aggregate the entries into a single position. For the job summary, I would list the type of work you did and the number of jobs. If you have had any noteworthy achievements during this time frame, create bullets for them. You do not need to have a bullet per job unless it was an exceptional achievement. This also works well for part-time jobs during college.

For every position, you use 2Qs for the scope, somewhere either in the description or the achievements. It gives the reader an idea of what you were dealing with during your time in that position. Remember, the idea is to differentiate yourself from others that did similar work.

Under each position, you add achievements. I would suggest two to four per post. If you have more, that is great, but make sure you are listing hard-hitting results. It would be counter-productive to make eight achievements, with most of them not showing much. Kind of cheapens the others.

Education

After your WORK EXPERIENCE, include your EDUCATION. This probably becomes less important, the lengthier your work history. Include any degrees or training that you believe would be beneficial to mention. For me, I no longer add this topic as most of my formal training was done many years ago.

> **TIP: If you have participated in any development of notable achievements in school that you would like to mention, list as the last entry under your WORK EXPERIENCE vice listing here. Except for class ranking.**

Usually, one line per item you list. Some people use two lines, one for the school and the next for degree type. I would not suggest putting in any GPA because that might work against you. Also, I do not believe it matters for most jobs. If you think it matters for your industry, then add if you wish.

Certifications

Next, you include CERTIFICATIONS if you have some that are not listed elsewhere. Any language testing could be listed here, as well. Note that some language certifications require scores. Include scores if you plan on using that as a selling point to getting a job.

Skills

Finally, you could include a list of qualifications for searching. I do not do this anymore, preferring to let my achievements speak for me. Whatever you do, please do not list every software item you know unless it is relevant to the targeted industry.

For IT jobs, I tend to look unfavorably on a resume that lists user productivity applications or home user operating systems. If you are going for a customer support position, then it could be relevant. For an engineering or programming position, stating you know how to use MS-Word, Outlook, Excel, PKzip, etc. would call into question your skills. People would think you are just listing everything you heard or have seen.

I would imagine this behavior is typical in many other fields. Make sure you do not list everything that has been seen. While it might get you attention, it is better to go deep rather than wide. If a potential interviewer first hits upon some areas that you barely know, there is a good chance they will end the interview or check out and not listen. Better not to imply you are knowledgeable in an area if you are not.

How far should I go back?

When considering what to keep or leave off your resume, think about the applicability to the job you are trying to get. Are the tools used anymore? I would suggest anything older than 20 years is probably not necessary to include unless you want to show some impressive achievements. The older the job, the less I would write about unless it is truly spectacular.

When I first left the military, I included each duty station with the things that I worked on and most of the training I had received. My resume was two pages then. Many jobs and years later, it is almost four pages with my military experience consolidated into a single entry with five bullets. The fourth page is about 2/3s of the way full. While writing this book, I have considered limiting the jobs from 2008 and back to just header and one accomplishment. To reduce the size of the resume.

There is no cut and dry about how long a resume should be. I suggest that if you make a paper copy that you keep it to less than four pages. More than that, and you might scare the reader. For electronic copies, I don't think there is so much a limit as much as ensuring that you have relevant data.

I looked at a friend's resume recently. He was an expert in his field and had about eight pages of data. It read more like a book, and while the achievements were impressive, it was just too long. I worked with him to shorten it, and we got it down to a little less than four pages.

We left out a lot of things he had on his original resume but made it less bookish and more short statements and hard-hitting bullets. He recently got a very prestigious job. Did I help? Maybe a little, but mostly it was a wealth of outstanding achievements. If anything, I just helped him make it easier to read.

But that is the goal of this book. You still need to have experience worthy of writing about, but I am hoping I can help you present it in the best way possible.

Wrap Up

So this is how I suggest putting together your resume. With the SUMMARY OF SKILLS, you give the reader a preview of what you are capable of that leads them further into your resume. Your WORK EXPERIENCE shows what, where, and how you worked and contributed to your positions.

The reader should have an idea of where you fit into their open position and how to rank you among the other potential candidates.

Job Search Tips

Chapter Three

In this section, I will try to cover some tips or ideas in the job-hunting process. These include thoughts on how to describe things on your resume to the interview.

Cover Letters

When should you use a cover letter? And how? I have mixed feelings about a cover letter. I must admit I have tried to use cover letters only a few times in my career, and I have never successfully had an interview with any of those companies. I do use recruiters, and they tend to be your cover letter.

While I am not a proponent of cover letters, I will tell you how I tried to write them. When I am trying to use a cover letter, I use them when I am not an excellent fit for the job. So that might have skewed my statistics on how successful they have been.

Usually, I try to explain why I believe I would be a good fit for their company. Referring to the achievements listed in my resume, I try to equate them with the main points of the job description.

Here is an example of how I tried to write one:

> I want to submit my resume for consideration for the Innovation Manager position in Tokyo, Japan. For the past 25 plus years, I have worked in many aspects of IT and pride myself on looking for

innovative ways to create, improve services, or reduce costs. I believe there is always a better way of doing something, but through hard-earned wisdom have learned that costs and timing are just as important.

As you will see in my resume, I have come up with ideas that are both within the IT field and entirely outside of it. One of the non-IT ideas was submitting new cabling (power and data cables) methods at <COMPANY NAME>, where I presented the idea to an internal "Shark Tank" innovation competition for one of the combat aircraft units. This idea made it to the next level, and if successful there, the company would seek patent protection.

Another idea is a recent one from <COMPANY NAME>. This one used drones in warehouses that <COMPANY NAME>'s senior executives have green-lighted for further development. I have come up with many ideas for this company, from transportation systems to medicine dispensers for the elderly.

I do not have in-depth healthcare industry knowledge but have previously tried to put together an alliance at <COMPANY NAME> for handling PAC imagery data. While not involving all aspects of the medical field, I did have to learn quite a lot about PACs and security requirements to propose the solution.

I also do not have a business-level understanding of Japanese but have worked through translators. Through these translators, I have submitted many business and solution proposals over the years.

While not perfect, my offer is an innovative person that has a knack for correlating unlike data types and finding opportunities. I welcome the opportunity to speak with you in person about my qualifications and how I can help your company further realize their vision.

As you can see, it was a stab at a medical industry position. I did not get an interview, but I tried to show that I was innovative.

Many blogs and books that discuss cover letters state that you should try to find the hiring manager's name to include that in the heading of the cover letter. I am not sure how important that is. At companies where I was a hiring manager, I was interested in reading their cover letter to see what they said, but I did not care who was the intended addressee. I read them through the internal HR job site. So is it essential to find that hiring manager? I would say, probably not.

Last thing on cover letters. I believe they are another opportunity to filter you out. If you have a lot of typos, that is bad. If you are talking about one type of job and I have a totally different one, I have to wonder would talking to you even be worth the effort. Maybe you don't want this type of job. You sounded so enthusiastic about the position you were describing in the cover letter.

So as I have said. Not a big fan and have not had any success. I definitely would suggest finding other sources about cover letters if you plan on using one.

What about significant time gaps between jobs

There has been a considerable time gap from your last job. How do you explain that? You can argue that it is not a new employer's business to know. That is true, but it is also equally valid that they do not have to hire you. Please remember, hiring managers are not only trying to find the right person, but they are also on the hook to make good choices in who they hire. Please understand, if you present them with an enigma, they most likely will pass on you for someone that does not offer a lot of questions needing answers.

You need to give them something to keep your candidacy moving forward. There is an excellent chance that if you have a lot of skills or achievements they like, a gap will not stop you from getting an interview. In the interview, you will most certainly get asked about it.

Honesty is the best policy, but you need to couch it in terms that explain it in the best light. If you were fired, you don't have to tell potential employers. Most countries make it a risky deal for former employers to provide negative information about a person. So there is little chance of them finding out, but you do need to give a reason. I can not give you ideas but suggest you practice your explanation.

What I can say is what I did when I was let go. That has happened twice. Once I was offered a package or a pay cut and the other time was over a disagreement with managing my team. Both times I was offered a severance package and took it. I am not one to work in an environment where I do not feel welcome.

With the first one, I also wrote my first book. I used that to explain my long period between jobs. It was true, and I was living off the severance and writing. If you have a hobby that has the potential to make money, you can say you were trying your luck at making that a career but figured out it was not going to work and came back.

If you took time off for parenting or caring for a family member, that is a good reason in a lot of people's minds. Use it, and it gives an excellent explanation for why you took the break.

Another good one would be furthering your education. Here you might need to show you got a certificate or class grade or something.

The one major thing with a long break is to be flexible in your expectations. If someone had a year or more break and did not show they continued their professional knowledge, I would be very hesitant to consider them for a senior position unless they have tons of experience within that field.

This is especially true in the world of technology. Things change so quickly that a year out could be a significant loss of knowledge on the latest gadgets. So be flexible getting back into the market.

A lot of jobs with little time at each one

The infamous job hopper. Is this the kiss of death to a candidate? It could be. What does it say about you? That is what you need to answer in the hiring manager's mind. Will you come and leave quickly, so she doesn't get what she needs? Remember, the hiring manager has a need that needs filling.

If you have a long history of job-hopping, that will work against you. Note, contract gigs are not considered job-hopping. Make sure you group these accordingly (refer to the Resume section about multiple jobs in one company).

If you do have many short term jobs that were not contracting, prepare an explanation. Also, if you had any significant contributions during that time, that would be good to list using 2Qs.

If your job-hopping was at the beginning of your adult life, things like a bunch of jobs in college might not be relevant. Even jobs right out of college could be ignored by saying you traveled the world or did something else.

Long periods of short jobs once you have established yourself would raise questions. These will need an explanation. What was going on when you jumped around?

Since moving to Japan, I have changed jobs on an average of every two years. Some would consider that job-hopping. Lucky for me, I have a list of accomplishments at each of these positions that makes me proud.

Here is a summary of how I have explained moves.

> *I came to Japan for personal reasons. My company in the States did not want to lose me, so they moved my position to Japan. I was with my company for almost two years in Japan when they started talking about outsourcing IT. I knew that my skills were not required in Japan, that they moved my position for me. This situation made me think that I would be one of the first that would be let go or have to take a significant pay cut.*

I moved to my second company at that time. Here I was outsourced to a large financial client. This went well, but most of the upward mobility opportunities would require me to move to Singapore. The reason I came to Japan was still there, so moving to Singapore (an 8-hour flight) was not acceptable. I went to this job with experiences in many aspects of network engineering. Reluctantly, large financial institutions tend to silo you. They pay very well for you to know your area of expertise. I found myself losing skills in other areas and didn't want to move to Singapore. So after two years, time to move.

My next company hired me as the cloud operations manager. So a step up in pay and title. I did this for two years and then moved into that company's sales team as a sales engineer for a newly started cloud sales team. Eventually, that team was absorbed back into sales, and I became a regular sales engineer. Reluctantly, I was an expensive sales engineer, still making my IT manager pay. This situation led to my first severance.

It took me almost a year to find a job. I was also writing my first book and can honestly say I was not looking hard for part of that time.

I found an opportunity with an international insurance company as a project manager and did that for almost a year. This was a contract job, and I didn't like the short term contracts and the worry that causes each time the end comes up.

Through my network, I found a long term contract IT manager position with potential for full time. Reluctantly, that didn't work out in the time frame I wanted. As luck would have it, I found a full time IT manager position.

So there you have my summary, up to my last job, that I tell potential employers. The idea is to provide a plausible reason for gaps and short term employment stints. No one is perfect, and if you try to build achievements wherever you go, people will be less inclined to judge you for gaps.

Interview hints

The interview. The thing you have been aiming for with your resume. What advice to give for an interview? This book is not about interviewing as much as getting your resume together, so I will just hit a few points here.

First, research the company. It doesn't matter if you targeted the company and built your resume around them, found a job description on a job site, or recruiter told you about the job. Research more to find out what the company does. Make sure you research the part of the company where you are going to be working.

I previously worked for Amazon's Web Service (AWS), which is part of Amazon but not. It is actually a subsidiary company of Amazon. I had a lot of people I interviewed think they were the same. When I asked them what do they know about AWS, most would talk about online shopping. That did not impress in regards to how I felt the candidate prepared for the interview.

Many large companies have subsidiaries. If you are going to work for the subsidiary, then make sure you know what they do. It probably does not hurt to know about the parent company either, but please make sure you know about where you will be working.

Also, prepare some questions that you would like to have answered. I want to ask about what projects or types of work I will do. I also like to bring them up throughout the interview and not always at the end. It helps to control the conversation, so you are not just in reactive mode. Also, people do like to talk about themselves and by extension, their company/work. If you have the interviewer talking as much as you or more is a good thing, it keeps the conversation engaging and shows you have an interest.

When I am doing this, I sometimes like to ask why they are doing something one way and not another. Or throw an anecdote on how I encountered the same problem or resolution. This also shows you know what the interviewer has gone through, so there is a good chance you can do the work.

Some companies like to work off standard questions, so this tactic might not work in those situations. In other cases, they want to come up with those really wild questions to see how you react. First, do not stress it. Answer the best way you can and move on. Again, company research might help you figure out if your target uses these tactics. Hint, Hint – research!

Overall, the idea is to make them think you can do the job and part of doing a job nowadays is being part of the team. If you come in quiet and shy or overconfident, then there is a good chance they will not pick you. Remember, you are selling yourself.

I once interviewed a person that was way overboard on his confidence. When I asked him some questions on what he can do, he would tell me, "No problem, I can do." I am not sure how many times I heard it during that interview, but it was enough for me to think he didn't know much and would probably wing it. I even made up something to see what he would say, and I got the same answer. Needless to say, he did not get a callback.

In some situations, you can be cocky and let your resume do the talking, but those times are not the norm. Why take a chance that you misjudged your skills and lost the opportunity because of bad behavior.

For interview dress, I always suggest business casual at the least for your attire. For some companies, a suit/formal might be too much, but I do not think it would be a negative. If you are not sure and worried, stop by the office and observe what people are wearing. If they are casual, then business casual. If they are in suits or all business casual, then formal.

No partying the night before, you would be surprised at how easy that can be picked up. Remember, they are watching you and concentrating on you. Regrettably, you would be surprised how many candidates do this. If you worked that day, make sure you are presentable when you get there. Find a bathroom and check yourself out. Again, you would be surprised at how many stains or lunch leftovers have found a way to secrete themselves on you. While your workday peers might not care much, it does detract from a first impression.

Finally, a thank you note. I have heard some people require this, and others couldn't care. I would be pleased to get one if you had my address, but it would not change my opinion on your fitness to take on the job. I have gotten most of my positions without thank you notes, but to be honest, I have no idea if I lost a job because I did not send one. So send via Email if you have their address. It's only a few minutes of your time, and you never know.

When should I tell my boss when I quit?

You are fed up with your work or your boss. Or you think you have a new job in the bag. What do you do? My advice is not to give notice until you have a start date. Once you get an offer, that is an excellent sign that the new company wants you. The problem is that it can still fall through if you have a background check.

Depending on the company, a background check can be very detailed or just a quick search for a police record. I do not know of any right way to determine which one will happen with any particular company. So until the background check passes, I would say you should not say anything to your current company.

If for no other reason than if something comes up on the background check, it might delay your employment start date for a while. Remember, once you submit your resignation, you should have a time in which you plan to leave the current company. Chances are the current company will not be flexible with that date. So wait until you have a firm confirmation of your start date and then draft your resignation.

Do I need to draft a resignation letter?

I have done this for most of my career. It seems the professional and proper thing to do. When you write a resignation letter, date it and mention the date you are leaving. Make a copy for your manager, yourself, and HR. You do not have to go in on why you are moving, and I usually say I appreciate what I have learned there and that I am leaving for further opportunities.

The reason I suggest writing out a resignation letter is that you have proof. I have heard of others that get asked to do more work, or can you quit next month instead of this month, etc. The letter to HR is to ensure your company understands its obligation. If only your boss has a copy, there is a chance he might try to pressure you into staying. I believe most bosses would not, but reluctantly, there are cases.

Your boss or others might ask you why or where are you are going. I do not believe any country requires you to answer this. You can, if you wish, but you are under no obligation.

One thing I have noticed is that not all companies will give you your full vacation time once you have given notice. In Japan, where I live, there is no law to require that. So think about this before quitting too. You might have to give up on some or a lot of your vacation time because they will not allow you to take it. This behavior might not always be a mean thing. If you give them two weeks' notice and have lots of things to teach your replacement, chances are they will not give you a lot of vacation time — business needs. So if you have a plan to leave, start taking your vacation days to "burn" them before you are ready to go.

What if they give me a counter-offer?

You meet the boss soon after submitting your resignation letter. He tells you how valuable you are to the company and offers to pay you more to stay. What do you do? Give him a number?

I would thank him and firmly tell him no. You have caught your boss unawares and in a bind. He has work that needs doing, and the one that knows how to do it is leaving. He is concerned with continuing the productivity of his work center.

There is a good chance that he will pay you what you want to keep you around until he is ready to have you leave. Now that you have said you are going, many bosses would consider you a traitor. Not exactly a nice thing to have to happen, but it does happen. So this means they are trying to delay your leaving until they have a replacement ready.

How bad could it be to stay and collect a bigger paycheck? Well, chances are it will not last a year before they have found your replacement. Please realize, this does not mean all cases will be like this, but there is a good chance that it will happen. Secondly, you probably already told the company that gave you an offer, no thank you.

If your company decides to get rid of you, then you will need to start the job search all over, and chances are the company that wanted you previously will have found someone else already or will no longer consider you a proper candidate. After all, you burned them.

Best to continue with your plans to leave.

Career Tips

Chapter Four

This section will cover some career tips that I have learned over the years. I hope they provide you some benefits as they have me.

Email address

Your Email address should be professional or at least neutral. Keep the funny named addresses for your personal use with friends. While it should not matter, it could negatively impact you. Remember, when hiring managers or HR gets a lot of resumes, they are looking for ways to narrow down the field. Don't let your Email address be the reason they put your resume to the side.

There are many free Email services to use, so it is pretty easy to get something. Make sure it is an account you can access regularly and that you can upload your resume through. Some services might not accept certain types of files, so be aware of any restrictions. Also, do not use your company's Email address on your resume or for correspondence with a job hunt.

Remember to check this Email address regularly, so potential offers do not go stale because you have not looked at the account.

It would be proper not to use this Email account for accessing other SNS services, especially if you enjoy getting into discussions of a non-professional nature on these services. Most SNS services require an Email address to register, and it would be easy to see what you are doing on that service. It is another way for someone to filter your resume out if you express opinions that they do not consider in line with their company. Why give them a reason to exclude you?

LinkedIn

If you are looking for a job, it would be advantageous to fill out your resume information in your LinkedIn profile. Many recruiters and potential hiring managers/HR check this service.

Make sure your profile picture also is professional or neutral. Some people do not use photos for their profiles. I think it best to put one on your account but do not see it as a negative if you do not. I am less likely to accept a connection request with someone without a profile picture. It just makes me feel more comfortable with one, and I imagine many others feel the same.

If you comment or post on LinkedIn, again remember to keep it professional and your comments non-controversial. Just another reason to exclude you from being selected.

Make sure you keep the data updated. For the current company, I usually list the job title, start date, and job description. Once I leave that company, then I would fill in achievements.

Does LinkedIn help? I think so. I found two jobs through the job listing on LinkedIn. One, my friend told me about the posting. The other I found just cruising the job postings on the site. I have also had a recruiter I met via LinkedIn, introduce me to a job.

Other job sites

Same as LinkedIn. Keep them up to date.

Social Network Sites (SNS)

If you like to get controversial, it might be best not to use your name. Some companies search the Internet for your name to see what you do. I have looked at LinkedIn to see if their profile can provide more insight into what I see in the resume. Some people go beyond that. As with other points, it doesn't help to give them a chance to say no.

Networking

Building your professional network never can hurt. You might hear of opportunities or even offered jobs. Always be professional, is a good rule for life. In my experience, I have encountered great people in my network. Many have become friends, and I cherish their friendship. Additionally, some have been great sources of information or inspiration, and I have occasionally gotten the word about job opportunities that I would not have known about without their 'heads up'.

On the flip side, you never know when someone that you had a problem with will be in a position to hurt your chances to get hired. I have been in situations and interviewed for opportunities that I knew someone in that job. I imagine my behavior at our previous meetings had an impact on whether I got the position or not. I assume my skills or lack of skills in that position also played a part, but people tend to go with someone that makes them comfortable.

This thought leads to the point about burning bridges.

Burning bridges

Not every job will end pleasantly. You might leave through no fault of your own. It happens, reluctantly, more often than we want. In my opinion, being angry about being made to go doesn't help your cause and could hurt. Bad bosses are out there, and sometimes you can't do anything about them. Try to leave as professionally as possible. People talk, and in some types of jobs, the circle of contacts is small. Best not to be the topic of discussion involving potential bosses or workers.

Another form of burning bridges comes in how you treat other workers or people you meet in your daily life. The way you treat people that do not directly work with you could be someone that is asked to give their opinion of you. This could be your fellow employees. If you treat other people at your company terrible, you never know when they might have an impact on the decision of who stays or goes. It is an excellent rule to live by to always be polite and professional to everyone you meet.

I was hiring for a position in Korea once, and something struck me weird about one of the candidates. She was technically proficient and could have done the job, but. We were in a conference room off the side of the reception area. Once we finished the interview, I walked out to the reception desk and asked the receptionist what she thought of the candidates that we had come in that day. I was pleasantly surprised that she gave some thoughtful and detailed observations. What I felt about that specific candidate was further backed up by the receptionist. The candidate was cold and demanding to the receptionist. That didn't seem desired for the position we were hiring. I made it a point to include asking those that come in contact with candidates for their observations.

Hiring pay

While most companies are different, there are some commonalities between most places. Most companies have pay ranges for each job level. From my experience, companies like to start people off in the middle of the range. This starting point gives people a chance to get raises without having to promote up right away.

When a company is going to extend you an offer for employment, they like to have your salary history. Most companies I have seen, like to offer a salary within a specific range of what you were previously making. This means that even if the job is offered in a particular range, they might provide you with less. Unless you wowed the hiring manager, you are likely to get near what you were making before.

It would be a good idea to try and find out the pay range for your job. Not sure this will always be possible, but if you find out what it is, you can figure out where you fall in that range, and it will give you an idea of what pay raises you can expect. If you are closer to the top of that range, chances are you will not get decent raises until you promote. It is what it is but good to know if you can find out.

Pay raises once hired

From my experience, most companies will not give significant raises unless that industry is booming. Typically, you have to promote or go to another company to get a substantial raise.

My first job out of the Navy got me some excellent pay raises. I believe I deserved it, but it also helped that the Internet Bubble was building to the Year 2000, and it was an employee's market. The first raise was pretty significant, and I was very appreciative. My manager told me that one of the main reasons I received what I did was because I was very dependable. I came in on time, didn't take time off a lot, and treated my co-workers and customers respectfully. Yes, there were other reasons for getting that raise, but it is informative how well a dependable worker can stand out. Be that person.

You will not always have those advantages, so be aware of the market. By being a hard worker and trying to seek out more than your job requires, you should generally be on management's mind (in a positive manner!). If you do not feel that is the case, first look at what you do. Are you trying to stand out positively? Are you trying to build your accomplishments? If not, then determine why not. If you don't like the job or are honestly trying and not succeeding, then consider moving on.

Toot your own horn

I always liked to believe that if I work hard, my boss will see that and reward me for the hard work. Reluctantly, most of the time, life does not work that way. There could be many reasons why this would not happen.

Your boss might not be an effective leader. They might feel writing up promotion justifications are a weak point of their skill set. Or if the promotion process is rigorous, they might not wish to put in, someone they perceive as a weak candidate. And your boss might have many 1 people they are watching and they do not have a good record of what you have achieved.

If you do not ask for it, you might not get it. To toot your own horn, you need to document what you do. As we have discussed in this book, create achievement summaries. These might not be ones that you can put in your resume, but they could be good enough for justification for your company. Now is the time when you pull out your achievement list. Write your promotion documents if you have the option. Do the leg work for your boss, and you will have some input on what passes for your justification.

If you keep a list of your accomplishments during your length of employment, it will help you create achievements for your promotion documents. When you write company achievements, pay attention to metrics. Since these are what the company measures your performance on, these are important to how they will value your contributions. If you have kept a running list, it should be mostly cut and paste to put into your company's promotion template.

Innovation

Find ways to innovate. Create new products, tools, or ways to improve your job. I would imagine that no job is perfect and can not be adjusted. Be the person that does this. Most of us love to complain about something, if not everything, about our jobs. Usually, everyone thinks someone else is already working on it, or it has already been brought up and shot down. The chances are that thinking is wrong.

Many innovations are not magic but just doing something in a different way. Be the person that suggests that. Peanut butter sandwiches and jelly sandwiches were probably already staples, but someone thought to combine them and look at the magic that created.

When innovating, you can't just mention the new idea. Most people will not believe it is possible or not see the value or don't want to do the extra work. The naysayers will come out of every dark corner or crevice to find problems with what you are suggesting. Be strong! You will need to draft the proposal and explain how it will work. Show how it is possible and the value to the company. If you believe it is possible, do the groundwork for the idea. While it might get shot down or found not useful for the company, it will show your management that you are thinking outside of the box and want to provide more value to the company. That can't be all wrong, and if nothing else, you can maybe add it as an achievement on your resume.

In a previous company, I came up with an invention that I was trying to get patented. I passed an internal innovation, Shark Tank-ish, process where I presented the design and how to use it. The committee members asked me to move forward with further building the idea and find a business unit to sponsor it, even told my management. Alas, that did not seem to matter to my management when considering my performance. They only cared about what was happening inside our organization, specifically employee survey results, and not other contributions to the company. This attitude has happened all too often in my career.

So there isn't much you can do about it other than keep doing your job as best you can and come up with ideas. Some managers think of their team's responsibilities to the exclusion of all else. If your management team does this and it stresses you out, then consider moving on to another more innovative company. If you can live with it or are happy to come up with ideas and not get credit, then stay if you wish. It can still work for your resume! I always want to find a place where I can do more than just the job description, and I will get recognition.

If you move on, make sure this new company is happy to have innovation from all employees and not just their engineers. Regrettably, I have been in companies that I thought were very innovative, but it seems that it is only if you are an engineer.

Going forward

Do you have the type of achievements that provide a significant impact? Feel like you are stuck in a job that you can't get ahead in? Don't despair.

One of the things you need to do is start building achievements. Only doing the job you are asked to do will probably keep you employed but might not get you recognized as someone worth promotion. In rough markets, it might not even save your job.

Business is in the business to make money. Even companies that get the idea that employees are valuable contributors to the success of the company want people that take the initiative. The more value you can show the company, the more likely you will be promoted and move up.

It is a fact of life. So how should you show initiative?

First, do your job as well as you can. We all get lazy or have bad days. The better you perform your duties, the less likely a bad day will be remembered. This is not a guarantee, but it is more likely that you will be given a little slack when you are having an 'off-day.'

Let's be honest. People that just do the minimum can bring down the rest of the team if they are allowed to do that without any consequences. Do not be one of those people. If you do not like the job, look for another but give the one you have your best efforts.

When hired, you are hired to do the job description and perform at a level on par with your peers. Chances are you will not be considered for promotion by just doing the job you are expected to do. This performance level also means you might not get more than the bare minimum raise for just doing the job. Would you consider someone that does only what is asked of them as someone for more work?

You need to be one of those that go beyond what is required. This initiative can take many forms, and you don't need to kill yourself to do it.

One way is to try and consistently do better than the average amount of work. Keep yourself in the upper 50% of your peers. This goal probably will not get you recognized, but it should keep you from being looked at negatively. Some companies evaluate the person at the bottom of the ranking in a negative manner. I have worked for some of these. The last ranked is marked for probation (called many things in many companies), that if their performance does not improve, then they are let go. I find that distasteful and even have argued against it but something that comes from much higher levels than I have ever been. Bottom line, I would highly suggest always to strive to be in the top 50% no matter what, as the minimum level of your performance.

Another way is to become involved in projects. Try to find ways to make significant contributions to the project. You do not always need to be the main person, but the more involved you are, the more management will positively think of you. Joining projects also helps to build your network with people that think positively of you.

One of the first jobs I had after leaving the Navy was in technical support. I worked on a sophisticated software application that was made by the company and also used there. When the network team asked for support, I was one of the ones that tried to help out. When it came time for our local network engineer to move to headquarters, I had a chance to move to the network team because I worked with them before. I wasn't the first choice, but I was considered and took the job. Because I helped, I had a chance in a job that I was only partially qualified. I had some Cisco network equipment experience, but I had experience with the monitoring tools like the application I supported. They took a chance with me because of the positive image they had of me.

Another way to contribute is to create documentation. Not all jobs have everything documented. If you see a need, try to fill it by creating what is needed. Everyone might not use it but get in the habit of it, and you never know. Maybe what you create will be used company-wide, and you will be considered a subject matter expert (SME) throughout the company. Something to gain you notice or, if nothing else, an achievement to put on your resume.

Along this line is become a mentor or trainer for new hires or other employees. Not only would this get you the label of an SME, but it could also open up another direction for your career to turn. Being a trainer would bring additional value to the company, and allow you to increase your network. Maybe even some travel to other sites.

When is it time to move on?

When is it best to consider a move? Besides the apparent themes of when you are not happy, lacking opportunity, or want more money? How about when you are doing the 9 to 5 grind?

When you have been in a job for a few years, and you really can't find achievements to put on your resume, it is time to consider a move. If you want to stay for retirement or don't care, fine, but realize that your plan might not match your management's plans. Sometimes just doing your job is not enough. As mentioned above, some companies negatively mark people who they consider the bottom of the team. Not that the person(s) did anything wrong; they just did less than everyone else.

If you find yourself in this position, consider finding a new job or revitalizing your current career. The longer you are in a situation where you do not have any significant achievements, the more likely that people will think that is negative.

This situation is especially true when job hunting. If you worked ten years at XYZ Corporation and have nothing but your tasks listed, I would probably put your resume aside and continue looking. I imagine most hiring managers would do the same.

What does that say about you? Unless the job is genuinely demanding, I imagine it would say you are happy to collect a paycheck and just do what is required to stay out of trouble. In other words, you lack initiative. Do hiring managers want to hire someone that they suspect will only do what they have to and no more? Hire someone that lacks ambition? For most jobs, I believe the answer is no. We want someone that will do well and contribute beyond their job description.

So how do you know when you are in danger of fitting this description. For one thing, you should keep your resume up to date. Or at least a list of achievements. If you find yourself not coming up with anything that you would consider worthy, then it is probably time to start planning a move. I would say if you have two years and nothing to write home about, then you are getting to that point.

Always look to see if there is something that needs doing. Most jobs have plenty of inefficient processes, find one to correct. I would argue that most of us have probably complained about a "stupid" process sometime in the last few months. Find these and figure out how to make the process better. Then you can propose a solution. It helps your current company and could be good resume candy.

Remember to think about 2Qs. How does it help? Can you quantify or qualify the results, the savings, or the impact? Make that your achievement.

If you can not or do not wish to find something in your current job, then get that resume out there. Either way, change up what you are doing to keep yourself "marketable" for the future.

Trying a new job field

So you are an expert in one area, and for some reason, you find yourself looking at a job with totally different skill sets. Or different enough that you feel you might have difficulties in competing against someone that knows that field. How do you fight?

Well, most jobs have a set of common skills. These are typically called soft skills, and they include people, social, and communication skills. These skills are pretty crucial for many types of jobs but probably will not get you hired alone.

If you are thinking of trying a job outside of your experience, it would be best to set your expectations appropriately. Chances are if you go into a completely different field, you will have to start near the bottom. The list of your experience and accomplishments might be pages long on your resume, but that doesn't equate too much to a hiring manager in a different field, unless you find a domain where you can lean on your previous experience.

If you were an IT guy for ten years and tried to get a job in sales or recruiting, chances are your previous experience would not mean much to the sales manager unless you are going into IT sales or recruiting of IT people. Then your experience could be essential because you can understand the lingo and feelings of your customers.

A good salesperson can probably sell anything with a basic understanding of the products. I believe they work from the position of finding the customer's problems and trying to solve them. Someone that was previously in IT would probably know the issues and would mention everyday experiences to build trust.

When I worked as a sales engineer, I had some great salespeople on my team. One would get us in and pretty much 'turn me loose' at the whiteboard. I would start talking about some of the common issues that the solution we were selling would fix or encounter. The 'tech' folks in the room would begin nodding, and soon we were having a tech discussion. It was a lot of fun.

This was also a job that I didn't have previous experience doing. I was the company's IT architect and operations manager for their cloud service. The salespeople would come to me for advice on how to sell the cloud service, and one thing led to another, and I had a chance to join a newly put-together cloud sales team as their sales engineer. That was a lot of fun and an excellent way to try another type of job that I did not have previous experience. In other words, sometimes it is good to 'take a shot' at something outside of your experience. You never know where that will lead you.

What if a job does not end well

Well, the worst happened. You were either fired or asked to leave. It has happened to me, and it can happen to you. If you were lucky, you might have seen that coming and have been actively looking for other work. If you did not see it coming, hopefully, you have an updated resume.

First, do no get down on yourself. Things happen, and sometimes you have a chance to change things, and other times you do not.

One of the reasons I suggest to keep one toe in the job market is for occasions like this. There is no guarantee you can find work or how quickly you can find employment. Especially the older or more senior you get. It is always best to look for a job when you have one. In this situation, we do not have that luxury. The focus is to get another job before you have too long of a break. For attitude, resume, and financial reasons.

There is a whole list of reasons why an extended break might not be best for you. I will leave those for someone else to talk about. What I want to discuss is how to look for that next job. First, do not financially ruin yourself looking for that perfect job. Remember, the job market does not guarantee an opening anywhere. What you think you might want might not be out there when you are looking. Be flexible.

Second, when companies say they want to know your salary history, they usually are doing that for the last job. The goal is to pay you around what you were making with a small bump. If you are unemployed, you do not have a pay scale they have to meet. They might offer you less thinking that you would be desperate to take it. Which you might be but try not to show it. Anyway, the key is to remember what you are making is what you will be judged upon when next you look for a job. If you are a senior person and take a junior position, then there is an excellent chance that the next company will look at you as a junior transitioning vice, a senior person that had to take a junior spot. Just think about that in your job search.

Third, you do not have to tell a prospective company that you got fired or were let go. I am not talking about lying, but you might want to practice your story to gloss over the reasons. It is not their business, but it is an understandable question. "You were doing good, then you left. Why?" It makes sense. So be prepared for this question. In most countries, they can not check, but the informal network can get word back via connections. So don't lie and prepare your story.

If you find yourself in the unlucky position of being out of work for a while, consider part-time employment. If you are senior, look at jobs where you can work a few days a week. It might not be used against you from a pay perspective at a new company, and it would show that you tried to do something. Volunteer work would be great, as well as looking for a field outside of your skill set.

I recently received a severance package from a company. During this time, I have found a part-time job working for an Audio/Visual company. Most of their products are starting to be networked, and that was a skill set their current employee base lacked. I negotiated that I would come in for two days a week to work for them. My objective is to get their people up to speed on networks, troubleshoot some customer issues, and help their product development. I am using my IT skills to help them while learning more about the AV world. They get an experienced IT network engineer with business and management experience on the cheap. It is fun, and I get to look busy on my resume.

If you can find something like this or volunteer in your area, great, remember to treat it like a full-time job. Make achievements, and it will look great on your resume as well as for your job satisfaction.

In my case, I am helping to build a digital signage solution integrating data from room reservations and workspace utilization tools. There are solutions out there, but many of them are custom jobs, and this would be something that uses well-known tools. I am excited to see it work and hope to get a few sales under my belt with it. If that is the case, that would be an achievement on my resume. Additionally, I am doing most of the product development on this idea by myself, along with creating sales documentation, marketing and support documents. Things I have not really done very much of in my previous jobs. I imagine I can really add to my resume with these new found skills and experiences. After all, how many people develop new products?

Look for opportunities and make it happen.

Conclusion

Chapter Five

With this book, I hope to give you the means to build a resume that shows how you have used your skills to provide value for your previous companies. By writing achievements, with 2Qs in mind, you will present the reader with a picture of what you accomplished in your previous jobs and give them a chance to project what you could bring to their company.

In the tip sections, we discuss ways to help you move forward in your career. Some are geared to help you create achievements using 2Qs, while others I have found help you be a more professional and productive person.

Is this exhaustive or the only way to do things? No, not by a long shot. These have worked for me, and I have been pretty successful at finding jobs and providing value to my companies. Hopefully, I have provided you some valuable tips that will help you become more confident and successful in your career.

In the Appendix, I provide a few of my resumes that I have used over my career. I will explain some of the differences in the Appendix. Some personal data as been omitted, but I hope you will see the progression of my thoughts on resume writing. Throughout my career, I have had excellent luck with getting interviews.

If you wish to know more of what I suggest or provide some feedback, follow my Facebook page (http://www.facebook.com/resumencareerbyjim). There I provide career and resume tips, with many responses to questions I answer on Quora.

Lastly, as most authors ask, I ask that you consider leaving a comment or rating on Amazon. It really does help move up the ranking and I would greatly appreciate it.

Appendix A

Resume from 1998

This is one of the first resumes I wrote when leaving the military. I believe it was the one that got me my first civilian job at Seagate Software in Orlando, Florida. I was not using a Summary of Skills, as I propose in the book, more a list of software and hardware that I knew. The bullets for my experience were pretty good in that I used 2Qs (didn't think of it as such then).

Since I was just getting out of the military, I expanded out each duty station as a separate Work Experience entry. After being out of the military for a while, I combined them then further consolidated them. For my military readers, notice how I tried to remove all military jargon but still tried to communicate the type of work I did. You will need to do this for your experience as well.

Personal Information (Centered)

SUMMARY

Information System specialist with 13 years experience in military communications, with the last five years, concentrating on LAN/WAN design and administration. Seeks position as a network administrator or integrator.

SKILLS

IntranetWare, NetWare 3.x, NT 4.0, Unix (Linux), Win95, Windows 3.x, DOS, CISCO Routers, TCP/IP, DNS, SMTP, NetWare/IP, NDS, cc:Mail products, MS-Office, Harvard Graphics, PC Repair, network design, network/system installation, help desk, WordPerfect, Bindview, modems, multiplexors, patch panels, network and communications troubleshooting, CNA 4.11, CNA 3.11, CNE Candidate.

PROFESSIONAL EXPERIENCE

1995-1998   Network Service & Support Branch Chief, NSGA Pensacola, Florida

Develops technical solutions to requests made by higher authority. Installs solutions and provides remote and on-site help desk support for all facets of field site's network.

- Project manager for the upgrade of 24 offices to IntranetWare. Connected 15 sites to organization's intranet.

- Co-developer and lead technician for integrating seventeen field offices into a classified WAN. Personally set up eleven sites within five months. Received award for performance during this project.

- Co-designed a remote dial-up solution allowing field offices corporate WAN access.

- Help desk coordinator for organization's 4500 users of NetWare and NT-based networks. Lead technician, resolved approximately 70% of calls received at center.

- Volunteer computer assistant for local American Red Cross Chapter (Pensacola, FL).

1992-1995   Campus Network Administrator, NCTAMS EASTPAC, Wahiawa, Hawaii

Provided guidance on IT matters to site managers, designed network expansion, help desk support for both local and remote users.

- Designed the expansion of a one server, 20-node network to a three server, 70-node network servicing three buildings and six remote sites. Supported more than 250 local and 150 remote users.

- Initiated the procurement of print servers, routers and repeaters that replaced older equipment or methods. Saved the department approximately $30,000 in maintenance and parts.

- Received award for performance as help desk coordinator, network security officer and office manager for a seven-person Information Systems office while acting as network administrator.

1991-1992   Communications Shift Supervisor, NCTAMS EastPac, Wahiawa, HI

Supervised a 12 person telecommunications shift handling communications for the eastern Pacific region.

- Oversaw the operation of over 300 telecommunications circuits and two mainframe messaging systems.

- Identified an alternate routing and storage procedure for handling electronic messages destined to remote subscribers utilizing PCs. Increased speed of service by 50% and reliability by 100%.

- Selected to relieve the departing network administrator due to technical and professional performance.

1989-1991   Communications Shift Supervisor, USS Blue Ridge (LCC-19), Yokosuka, Japan

Supervised a three person afloat communications center handling HF and satellite communications.

- Selected to represent site as the fleet subject matter expert at a world-wide communications conference.

1987-1988   Senior Communications Operator, NSGA Kami Seya, Japan

Maintained telecommunication circuits, performed operator tasks on mainframe message systems and handled cryptographic material and equipment. Kept communications event logs.

1985-1986   Junior Communications Operator, NSGA Hanza, Okinawa, Japan

Maintained telecommunication circuits, performed operator tasks on mainframe message systems and handled cryptographic material and equipment. Kept communications event logs.

1984-1985   Recruit, Training Commands at Pensacola and Orlando, Florida

Learned basic military and communications theory and procedures.

CLEARANCE

Has held a TOP SECRET/Special Intelligence clearance with Special Background Investigation for the last 13 years.

CERTIFICATION

1997	Novell Certified NetWare 4.11 Administrator (CNA)
1994	Novell Certified NetWare 3.11 Administrator (CNA)

EDUCATION

1997	NetWare 4.11 Adv Admin Course, Networks of Florida
1997	MS Windows NT 4.0 Server Course, New Horizons
1996	NetWare 4.1 NDS Design and Implementation Course, New Horizons
1996	Novell's Networking Technologies, NTTC Corry
1996	NetWare 4.1 Basic Admin Course, NTTC Corry
1995	Navy school. Network Administrator, University of West Florida
1994	National Security Agency Course: Operational Information Systems Security
1993	NetWare 3.11 Adv System Manager Course, ISTC Pearl Harbor
1993	NetWare 3.11 System Manager Course, ISTC Pearl Harbor
1986	Navy School: Tactical Communications Systems, NTTC Corry
1985	Navy School: Basic Communications Theory, NTTC Corry

Resume from 2004

I made this resume while living in Orlando, Florida. This is probably more an example of not following my advice. I put together this resume to try and find a job in Japan. As you can see, the format changed. I did get a few hits, but my company eventually agreed to move my position to Japan.

I think I was following the advice of the day. Most 'experts' were advising to list what you do, but as you can see, many of those statements are ones that almost anyone in the field can say. People that did not know who Veritas Software was would not have known the size or work style. Also, I was listing the majority of equipment I worked on but did not say how often, to what level, or how I implemented them. For all, a reader would know is that I racked and stacked them only, which was not the case.

Personal Information.

Objective: Well-rounded network engineer with a strong emphasis on network monitoring and data analysis looking for a LAN/WAN network engineer position.

Summary of Skills:

- Managed telecommunications and IS work centers consisting of up to 12 people.

- Network engineer using Cisco routers, switches, firewalls, VPN and wireless devices.

- Designed and managed an S&P 500 company's network performance monitoring systems.

- Designed, installed and configured small office to campus level TCP/IP based networks.

- Administered NT, Solaris, Linux, HP-UX and Netware systems.

- CCNA, CNE (4.x), CNA (3.x-4.x), Certified NerveCenter Administrator

- Held a TOP SECRET/SBI security clearance for entire naval career.

Work Experience:

Veritas Software: Heathrow, Florida   Mar98 – Present

(June 2000 – Present) Senior Network Engineer, Global Infrastructure Group

WAN: Performs maintenance, design, installation and troubleshooting on ATM, ISDN, VPN, Frame Relay, PTP and MPLS links. Recognized for successfully implementing a

VoIP-enabled infrastructure for an overseas call center.

LAN: Manages Cisco switch-based networks throughout the company. Of note, rewarded for key role played in successful relocation of a regional data center and associated WAN links, a major software development group and an inside sales call center; all with negligible network downtime.

Monitoring: Initiated a project to create a corporate-wide monitoring system vice one tailored to a single group's needs. Previous to this project, the company had no central monitoring or notification system. Performed most project related work; from gathering requirements and selecting vendors; to installing and configuring servers, applications and standing up corporate NOC. Increased monitoring from just monitoring bandwidth and system health to include application response, path response and traffic analysis.

Technologies used: MicroMuse NetCool, CiscoWorks 2000, Concord eHealth Suite, NetScout RTM and Performance Manager, Open NerveCenter, Solaris 2.6-2.8, NT 4.0, Win2k, Lucent QIP, Etherpeek, Remedy AR, Visio, NetScout RMON probes, Cisco routers (c7xxx/c36xx/c26xx/c25xx), Cisco Catalyst switches (35xx/4xxx/5xxx/6xxx), Cisco CallManagers, VPN Concentrators and PIX firewalls, DNS, SNMP, TCP/IP, EIGRP, Perl, SQL

(1998 – 2000) NerveCenter Senior Support Specialist, Technical Support

Provided technical support to various Fortune 500 companies using the NerveCenter product. Assisted customers with integration and configuration issues. Provided input to the product design and assisted with quality assurance testing before release. Due to knowledge of product and troubleshooting skills was selected to provide on-site assistance to NerveCenter customers. Knowledge of the above products and Cisco routers led to a position in the Global Infrastructure Group.

Technologies used: MicroMuse Netcool, Seagate Software NerveCenter, HP Openview and ITO, CA Unicenter, Tivoli TME10, Perl, SNMP, TCP/IP, Unix shell scripting, Solaris 2.5-8, HP-UX 10, NT 4.0, Cisco 2511 routers, DNS, SMTP

United States Navy, 1984 – 1998

(1995 – 1998) Network Service and Support team lead; Naval Security Group Activity Pensacola, Florida. Project manager and lead technician for organization's core network team. Designed a Novell Intranetware NDS tree for a 17 site, 4500+ user organization. Installed and configured Novell file servers, designed physical network layout and configured Linux gateways that acted as SMTP relays and DNS servers. Also performed as organization's 2nd level help desk coordinator and lead technician, resolving over 65% of center's calls.

(1992 – 1995) Network Administrator; Naval Computer & Telecommunications Area Master Station, Hawaii. Network administrator for a 3 building, 250+ local and 100+ remote user network. Performed as server administrator, help desk technician and network security officer. Received award for superior performance and was requested to transfer to the organization's core network team in Pensacola.

(1991 – 1992) Communications Shift Supervisor; Naval Computer & Telecommunications Area Master Station, Hawaii. Supervised a 12 person shift, consisting of a mainframe message processing center; a circuit facility control center; and an HF and satellite broadcast message center. Outstanding performance and knowledge of communications led to selection as site's network administrator.

(1984 - 1991) Various Naval Commands. Performed the duties of a Cryptologic Technician Operator. Experience includes message preparation; maintaining encrypted HF, UHF and satellite communications; mainframe system operator and the handling of cryptographic keying material. Ability to grasp technology's impact is highlighted by the selection as subject matter expert to represent the theater commander for a world-wide ship-borne naval communications conference.

Training:
- Cisco IP Telephony (CIPT), Automated Research Systems
- Concord eHealth Developers Training, Concord Communications
- Cisco Enterprise Management Solutions, Global Knowledge
- Cisco Interconnecting Cisco Network Devices, Global Knowledge
- MicroMuse NetCool/Omnibus user/sysadmin/advanced, Adage Networks
- CA Unicenter Fundamentals, Computer Associates
- HP Openview v5.0 NNM Fundamentals/Management, Hewitt Packard
- Sun Solaris 2.7 Sysadmin 1 & 2, Global Knowledge
- Microsoft SQL v6.5 Database Administrator Course, Seagate Software
- Seagate Software NerveCenter Administrator, Seagate Software
- NetWare 4.11 Administration Course, Networks of Florida
- Microsoft Windows NT 4.0 Server Course, New Horizons
- NetWare 4.1 NDS Design and Implementation Course, New Horizons

- 8 week Navy school: Network Theory and Application, University of West Florida
- National Security Agency: Operational Information Systems Security
- NetWare 3.11 System Manager Course, Navy on-site
- Navy School: Tactical Communications Systems, Navy on-site
- Total Quality Management, Navy on-site
- Leadership Development Program, Navy on-site
- Workcenter Safety Supervisor Certification, Navy on-site

Resume from 2010

Many years later, I created this resume. This was after I came to Japan and had a job change. I went back to the bullet format for Work Experience and removed the training section since most of that was a long time ago.

I also shortened many of these bullets and add more 2Qs into them. Many of them are explaining the projects and wasting space. I imagine I can get this down to two pages quickly by adhering to this book.

Personal Information

OBJECTIVE: Network professional with proven success and recognition promoting innovative ideas and meeting business needs, seeks a network engineer position.

SUMMARY OF SKILLS:

- Performed as 2nd level tech support engineer for NerveCenter, an snmp event correlation engine.
- Network experience ranging from managing data center moves, designing third party network connections to troubleshooting WAN and firewall connections.

- Network monitoring expert. Set up and administrated an S&P 500 corporation's fault and capacity management system.

- Experienced in Unix (Solaris, HPUX, RedHat), Windows, NetWare.

- Experienced in BlueCoat Proxy Systems, NetScout RMON probes, Cisco PIX, ASA and Call Manager applications; Juniper WXC/Peribit WAN Optimization devices and Netscreen firewalls.

WORK EXPERIENCE:

BT Japan LTD: Mar08 – Present

Network Engineer, Global Financial Services

Tokyo, Japan

Assigned to the Credit Suisse account, responsible for network implementations primarily in Tokyo and Seoul. Responsible for design and development of router and switch expansions, blade chassis and third party network (TPNC) implementations. Perform as 3rd line support for Credit Suisse's Tokyo NOC.

- Lead engineer for Tokyo office expansion. During the 8 month project; designed a floor addition, orchestrated the network changes for approximately 750 user moves between floors and designed a highly resilient 200+ trader network expansion of the trading floor without major disruptions to the Tokyo office operations.

- Lead engineer for Osaka Stock Exchange (OSE) co-location facility project. The client wanted to build a presence in the OSE's co-location data center to benefit from low-latency trading. Designed the connectivity, configured network equipment, firewalls and installed at the Osaka facility.

- Led the migration project for upgrading the BlueCoat proxy systems in Tokyo. Developed the migration plan for 120+ applications for a 700+ user base. Migration was successfully implemented without major issues.

Symantec Corporation: Mar98 – Feb08

(2006 – Present) Network Engineer, Global Infrastructure Service

Tokyo, Japan

Network engineer primarily responsible for the company's growing Asian-Pacific infrastructure. Maintains router and switch configurations, provides network architecture and installation services and troubleshoots LAN/WAN problems.

- Lead network engineer on the consolidation of offices in Seoul, Beijing, Chengdu and Tokyo. Designed and installed the networks, utilizing Cisco Catalyst 6500 switches, c3845 ISR routers for MPLS wan connectivity with DMVPN encryption tunnels. Seoul was noted as "This is the smoothest move in a long time", Andy McConnell, Senior Manager, Global Infrastructure Services.

- Identified and designed the implementation of Alterpoint's Device Authority, a change and configuration management tool. Drafted ROI statements, evaluated, installed and configured the application. Added the devices and trained team members in the tool's use. Primary evangelist for the product.

- Architect and primary engineer of Juniper WXC wan compression implementation for the company. Developed QoS and application configurations for the WXC devices. Some sites recording performance increases of 3 to 8 times physical bandwidth. Manages the Juniper WXC element management application, CMS.

- Designed a method to use a single VPN profile throughout the Asian region for wireless and guest network connections, using Cisco ASA security devices. This resulted in simplifying the user's experience by requiring only a single VPN profile.

(2000 – 2006) Network Engineer, Global Infrastructure Service

Heathrow, Florida

Network engineer responsible for managing the corporate network infrastructure, primarily, in the United States. As team's system administrator, maintained the corporate fault and performance monitoring systems. As a network engineer, maintained router and switch configurations, provided network architecture and installation services and troubleshot LAN/WAN problems.

- Critical to the successful implementation of an international VoIP-enabled technical support call center. Issues included us being one of Cisco's first ATM IMA interface customers requiring extensive troubleshooting. Rewarded for contributions made to this project.

- Re-engineered network infrastructure to move a regional data center and major call center to new buildings. Designed network infrastructure using Catalyst 6509 switches and dark fiber between buildings. Recognized for key role played that allowed these business units to operate with minimal impact during the move.

- Lead network engineer for company's acquisition projects. Managed the integration of three companies. Resolved design issues between the acquired companies and Symantec.

- Core team member for DMVPN MPLS implementation of corporate offices in the US. Configured BGP, new routers and other network devices at each site.

- Solely responsible for the selection, design and implementation of the company's first corporate-wide fault and performance monitoring solution. Designed notification systems, developed operator guides and customized display views.

- Efforts in traffic analysis and capacity planning reduced projected bandwidth costs by identifying unauthorized use of the networks or helping customers determine a more efficient use of existing bandwidth.

- Managed Cisco VPN concentrators and Pix firewalls for internet segments and datacenter zone separation. Used Solsoft's Policy server application to manage the Pix firewalls.

(1998 – 2000) NerveCenter Senior Support Specialist, Technical Support

Heathrow, Florida

Provided configuration and customization support to customers of the NerveCenter product line.

- Resolved customer issues with NerveCenter, Openview, NetView, NetCool and Unicenter integration, server OS and NerveCenter behavior model development.

- Utilized Perl, IP, SNMP and knowledge of other products to support customer implementations of NerveCenter. Common customer issues involved database access, knowledge of network devices and servers, Perl scripting, packet analysis and general knowledge of TCP/IP communications.

- Technical expertise and professional attitude led to selection for customer (AOL) on-site support visit. AOL had a critical issue jeopardizing further software purchases. Defused situation and assisted NerveCenter engineering team with further troubleshooting.

United States Navy, Cryptologic Technician Operator 1984 – 1998

(1995-1998) Network Service & Support Branch Lead Technician,

NSGA Pensacola, Florida

Led engineer for Naval Security Group's global networks. Managed a global NetWare NDS structure, WAN connectivity and cc:Mail systems. Designed networks, configured servers and resolved user issues.

- Co-architect and lead technician for integrating 17 field offices into a classified WAN. Received award for performance during this project.

- Help desk coordinator for 4500 users of NetWare and NT-based networks. Lead technician, resolved approximately 70% of calls received at center.

- November 1997 evaluation stated: "Naval Security Group's resident expert on networking and Novell NetWare. Displayed exceptional technical skills and resourcefulness..... Developed solution for WEBWORLD Phase II, providing remote sites dial-up NSA network access...."

- Co-developed Linux-based routers that acted as a mail gateway and DNS server for use at remote sites; this was required due to low budget limits in the initial stages of the project.

(1992-1995) Campus Network Administrator, NCTAMS EastPac, Wahiawa, HI

Managed a three-building, Netware based, classified campus network.

- Received award for performance as network security officer and office manager for a seven-person Information Systems office while acting as network administrator.

(1991-1992) Communications Shift Supervisor, NCTAMS EastPac, Wahiawa, HI

Supervised 12 person telecommunications shift handling communications for the eastern Pacific region.

- Selected to replace the departing network administrator due to technical and professional performance.

- Developed a method to store remote customer message traffic electronically while customer was off-line. This method drastically increased speed of service upon customer service resumption.

- Recognized for leading the communications shift with the fewest errors and best performance of four sections.

(1985-1991) Communications Operator, Various US Navy sites

Maintained telecommunication circuits, performed operator tasks on mainframe message systems and handled cryptographic material and equipment.

Resume from 2019

This is my current resume but does not include the writing of this book. I did remove the Objective, as it is not that effective in my opinion. I think many years ago, it was something to consider when people were handed paper copies of resumes, but not in the world of the Internet.

Additionally, some of the older entries have been pruned of bullets to reduce the size. The next version will probably see most of the Navy, Symantec, and BT entries pared down. They are pretty old, and as I am trying to start a new career (or something), they are not really relevant when I tried to work in the same field. I have kept some of the statements under the Navy that I have mentioned in the Summary of Skills.

SUMMARY OF SKILLS:

- Managed an international IT operations team, cloud data center teams and naval special intelligence communications shifts.

- WAN and LAN architect/engineer experienced in trading floor buildouts, global MPLS WANs, High Frequency - Trading networks, compute farm networks, virtual desktop initiatives, data center moves and office buildouts.

- Managed cloud service data centers with up to one thousand racks and up to 24,000 physical servers under management.

- Over 25 years of IT and communications experience in management, IT architect, data center management, network security officer, network and system administration to technical support.

- Designed and managed the fault and capacity management system for an S&P 500 corporation.

- Experienced at analyzing and correlating data, with a knack for discovering inefficiencies that can save money.

- Cisco Certified Network Administrator, ID: CSCO10651541 - June 2003.

- VMware Technical Sales Professional 5 – October 2013

- Almost 14 years of U.S. Naval service with a TOP SECRET/Special Background clearance.

- Wrote and published a fictional book.

WORK EXPERIENCE:

Vega Project K.K. - April 2019 – Present

Tokyo, Japan

Technical Consultant

Contract. Provide IT and product support to team for new IP network based products.

- Created digital signage solution called In-House Digital Signage (IHDS), that integrates internal tool data with general communications for employee information sharing. Initiating sales training at time of writing.

Amazon Web Services Japan – April 2017 – February 2019

Manager, Data Center Operations

Tokyo, Japan

Managed fourteen people at two data centers responsible with over 24,000 servers in the fourth largest cluster globally.

- Recognized the need for team work between data centers, hosted forums for members to come together to discuss experiences and receive training. Positive feedback from attendees and management. Regional management asked to expand this across Asia.

- Developed concept to create a secure means to handle and track used storage media within data centers. Currently in the prototyping stage. The idea received a regional Kaizen award.

- A lead contributor to Amazon's internal innovation sites (ideas, comments and judging). At time of this writing, ranked number two having submitted numerous ideas that have passed initial vetting and have been turned over to development teams.

- Submitted an idea about drone usage in warehouses that was selected to be further developed, as a finalist idea in the annual company-wide innovation competition for 2018. One of 289 ideas from nearly 3000 that was judged and selected by the senior leadership team. Submitted 9 additional ideas and ranked 22 of 578 volunteer judges for the competition's initial judging phase.

Boeing Japan – September 2015 – March 2017

Manager, Regional IT Operations for Japan, Korea and Taiwan

Tokyo, Japan

Contract. Managed an operations team of ten supporting all Boeing endeavors, at over 40 sites, in this region. Support entails desktop support, local IT hands-on support, project management and IT asset acquisition for Boeing's commercial and defense related activities.

- Created an environment of fiscal responsibility among team members that resulted in identifying cost savings in contractual services that already have amounted in a reduction of 40,000 USD per year.
- Identified possible Boeing International savings of up to 4 million USD in laptop maintenance fees by analyzing the repair/replace rate. Proposal was being evaluated at departure.
- Submitted damaged cable detection solution invention that uses photon emissions.
- Led an effort to consolidate the ownership and management of IT services offered throughout Asia into a centralized data center in Tokyo. Effort will ensure better customer and vendor relations in region.
- Maintained 100% retention rate, one of the highest customer satisfaction rates and had two members promote up to other positions in Boeing.

Hays Staffing & Recruiting – October 2014 – September 2015

Project Manager

Tokyo, Japan

Contract. Managed AXA-Tech/AXA Life Japan's Office 365 migration project for 11,000+ mailboxes. The project consisted of migrating to Office 365 from a hosted exchange solution with Symantec's Enterprise Vault.

- Through data analysis of mail usage records, discovered and proposed cost savings up to 40 million JPY per year.
- Led the project as technical project manager since company did not have a local mail team.

Author February 2014 – Present

Wrote and published, Wall of Destruction, a When Atlantis Fell novel. (Oct, 2014)

KVH LTD – May 2010 – January 2014

(May 2012 – January 2014) Senior Specialist, Solutions Architect, Sales Division

Tokyo, Japan

Designed solutions for customers related to KVH products (data center, networks, IaaS, managed services and storage). Provided solutions, drafted proposals and led technical discussions with customers.

- Well versed in IT; worked on numerous opportunities that range from selling co-location, WAN design, BCP solutions, up to petabyte backup/archive solutions, video surveillance, VDI and DC virtualization designs for customers of many industries in Japan and throughout Asia.
- Worked on opportunities ranging from a few thousand dollars to a few million dollars in monthly revenue.
- Wrote on KVH's corporate blog about technical or industry matters. This also included providing tweets for the corporate account. One of the leading providers of material.
- Guided partners to build an analytical ecosystem built around analyzing video and other forms of data for business intelligence needs as well as security. KVH would provide the infrastructure of the service.

(May 2010 – May 2012) Service & Technology, OSS/IT Architect – Manager

Tokyo, Japan

Multiple concurrent positions: IaaS Data Center Manager and OSS/IT Architect

Hired as KVH's IaaS data center and cloud support manager. During company's reorganization, became the OSS/IT architect and continued to perform in the previous roles.

- Oversaw the build out of KVH's new headquarters in Tamachi, (Tokyo,Japan). Managed the IT network implementation and coordinated services with other teams to move over 300 people to the new office.
- Oversaw the build out of KVH's first IaaS data center (200 racks). Managed the cloud operations team responsible for on-boarding and production support to customers and ensuring the ongoing readiness of the cloud service.

- Managed the consolidation and move of KVH's network operations centers (NOC) and operations group into our headquarters. This group consists of over 120 technicians located at multiple sites around Tokyo, managing KVH's infrastructure and 1500+ customers. This project was accomplished on-time and under budget with no drop of coverage.

- Architect for OSS/IT systems. Led projects for network and server consolidation, remote site build outs, an enterprise backup solution, a telepresence solution, a new corporate monitoring solution and remote access/virtual desktop solution using Citrix's XenDesktop/XenApp solution.

BT Japan LTD: March 2008 – April 2010

Network Engineer, Global Financial Services

Tokyo, Japan

Assigned to the Credit Suisse account for network implementations primarily in Tokyo and Seoul. Responsible for design and implementation of router and switch expansions, blade chassis and third party network (TPNC) implementations. Perform as 3rd line support for Credit Suisse's Tokyo NOC.

- Lead engineer for Tokyo office expansion. During the 8 month project; designed a floor addition, orchestrated the network changes for approximately 750 user moves between floors and designed a highly resilient 200+ trader network expansion of the trading floor without major disruptions to the Tokyo office operations.
- Lead engineer for Osaka Stock Exchange (OSE) co-location facility project. The client wanted to build a presence in the OSE's co-location data center to benefit from low-latency trading. Designed the connectivity, configured network equipment, firewalls and installed at the Osaka facility.
- Led the migration project for upgrading the BlueCoat proxy systems in Tokyo. Developed the migration plan for 120+ applications for a 700+ user base. Migration was successfully implemented without major issues.

Symantec Corporation: March 1998 – February 2008

(2006 – Feb08) Network Engineer, Global Infrastructure Service

Tokyo, Japan

Network engineer that managed the company's growing Asian-Pacific network infrastructure.

- Lead network engineer in the consolidation of offices in Seoul, Beijing, Chengdu

and Tokyo. Seoul was noted as "This is the smoothest move in a long time", Andy McConnell, Senior Manager, Global Infrastructure Services.
- Identified and designed the implementation of Alterpoint's Device Authority, a change and configuration management tool. Primary evangelist for the product.
- Architect and primary engineer of Juniper WXC WAN compression implementation for the company. Developed QoS and application configurations for the WXC devices. Some sites recording performance increases of 3 to 8 times physical bandwidth.

(2000 – 2006) Network Engineer, Global Infrastructure Service

Heathrow, Florida

Network engineer that managed the corporate network infrastructure, primarily, in the United States.

- Re-engineered network infrastructure to move a regional data center (100+ racks) and major call center to new buildings. Recognized for key role played that resulted in minimal impact during the move.
- Solely responsible for the selection, design and implementation of the company's first corporate-wide fault and performance monitoring solution.

(1998 – 2000) NerveCenter Senior Support Specialist, Technical Support

Heathrow, Florida

Provided configuration and customization support to customers of the NerveCenter product line.

- Resolved customer issues with NerveCenter, Openview, NetView, NetCool and Unicenter integration, server OS and NerveCenter behavior model development.

United States Navy, Cryptologic Technician Operator 1984 – 1998

Various US Navy sites and ships.

- Co-architect and lead technician for integrating 17 field offices into a classified WAN. Received award for performance during this project.

- Received award for performance as network security officer and office manager for a seven person Information Systems office while acting as the network administrator for a classified campus network.

- Supervised 12 person telecommunications shift handling communications for the eastern Pacific region.
- Maintained a TOP SECRET/Special Intelligence clearance with Special Background Investigation for entire naval career.

www.ingramcontent.com/pod-product-compliance
Lightning Source LLC
Chambersburg PA
CBHW030951240526
45463CB00016B/2447